Homemade
Cakes

Homemade
Cakes

Philippa Vanstone

MQP

Published by MQ Publications Limited
12 The Ivories, 6–8 Northampton Street
London N1 2HY
TEL: +44 (0)20 7359 2244
FAX: +44 (0)20 7359 1616
EMAIL: mail@mqpublications.com
www.mqpublications.com
Copyright © MQ Publications 2005
Illustrations copyright © Penny Brown 2005

ISBN 1-84072-629-6

Printed in China

Recipe text copyright:

pp. 14, 15, 16, 17, 18, 21, 23, 24, 26, 32, 39, 41, 42,
44/5, 47, 51, 52, 55, 57, 60, 61, 66,
67, 68, 73, 75, 78, 83, 84, 89, 90, 91, 96,
98/9, 101, 102, 103, 104, 105, 106, 108, 109 ©
Philippa Vanstone 2005. pp. 20, 29, 33,
34, 40, 54, 58, 59, 72, 82, 86, 87 © **Maggie
Mayhew** 2001, 2003. pp. 25, 28, 50, 106 ©
Caroline Barty 2001, 2002. pp. 36/7, 70/1 ©
Liz Wolf-Cohen 2001, 2002. pp. 64, 92/3 ©
Susan Wolk 2000. pp. 65, 76/7 © **Carol
Tennant** 2001, 2003.

Text and covers
are printed on
100% recycled paper.

Contents

Introduction

There is nothing more welcoming than the smell of a freshly baked homemade cake, and this book contains a huge variety of cake recipes for bakers of every ability—whether a novice or veteran cake maker there is something for everyone. From exotic cheesecakes or rich and tempting chocolate cakes, to sophisticated desserts, over-the-top celebration cakes, or simple and tasty sponges to serve with coffee—the list is endless.

A large number of these recipes are well-established and much-loved American classics that have been passed down by family members from generation to generation, but there is also a delicious selection of less well-known cakes to try. The book covers a wide range of occasions, whether it's the holiday season, an impromptu coffee morning for friends, a children's birthday, or an important dinner party where you're trying to impress, you'll never be stuck for ideas again.

It's simply a case of banning the kids from entering the kitchen, putting on your apron, rolling up your sleeves, and baking cakes just like Grandma used to make!

You'll soon be whipping up traditional and much-loved family recipes while adding new and improved favorites to their list. There is something deeply satisfying and soothing about making your own cakes. A homemade cake baked with fresh, quality ingredients undoubtedly tastes better than any of the store-bought varieties you can lay your hands on and cake baking equipment is readily available and easy to come by. Guests will always appreciate the extra effort that's involved when you serve them up a moist, thick slice of heavenly homebaked cake. So go on, spoil your friends and family and make Grandma proud!

Tips for Succesful Cake Making

Equipment

Cake pans and tins: Round pans come in a range of sizes. The most useful ones are 8in/20cm and 9in/23cm, although 10in/25cm is also often used. Loose-bottomed pans make turning out the cake much easier, and springform cake pans are useful for delicate cakes that cannot easily be turned upside down to remove them from the pan. Square and long pans are used for large cakes; they are especially useful for families. A pan measuring 9 x 13 x 1½in/23 x 33 x 4cm deep is a good standard size. A 2lb/900g loaf pan is also useful to have, as is a Bundt pan, which is a deep pan with a tube in the center. A size 102 is a versatile size.

Other useful equipment: Measuring cups for both dry and liquid measures and an accurate pair of scales are essential if you want to obtain good results from your baking. A hand-held mixer is timesaving and also vital for many recipes. Whisks, wooden spoons, a small pastry brush, a rolling pin, and a set of different-sized mixing bowls are also useful for most recipes. A food processor can make quick work of many recipes.

Essential Ingredients

The key ingredients for cake making are flour, raising agents, sugar, eggs, and fats: butter, oil, and margarine.

Flour: Most recipes in this book use all-purpose flour or self-rising flour, although cake flour, which has a lower protein content, is best used for making cakes that don't require the strength of all-purpose flour. If you are unable to get cake flour you can cut all-purpose flour with a little cornstarch; use as little as 1 tbsp for every 2 cups/300g of all-purpose flour.

Sugar: Superfine sugar will always give the best results in baking.

Baking powder: and baking soda are chemical raising agents for cake making.

Eggs: Try to choose free-range eggs.

Chocolate: Always choose the darkest chocolate with the highest percentage of cocoa solids, as this will give the most intense flavor.

Fats: Use good quality butter, oil, and margarine for the best flavor. Many of the recipes specify sweet butter for using with cakes.

Making the Cake Batters

The main methods used in cake making are creaming, whisking, melting, and rubbing-in.

Creaming: Butter and sugar are blended or beaten to incorporate air and to create a smooth, softened mixture that is pale in color and light in texture.

Whisking: incorporates air into the cake.

Melting: Several ingredients are heated together gently to give a homogenous liquid. This method is mainly used for making frostings.

Rubbing-in: This method is used for making cookies, toppings, and some cakes.

Folding or combining ingredients: should be done with a light hand. Using a large whisk and lifting the whites or cream through a mixture helps to retain the incorporated air. When folding flour through a wet mixture use a metal spoon, as this will displace the least amount of air, helping to preserve the lightness of the cake.

Baking

Always preheat your oven to the correct temperature before starting and put the cake batter straight into the oven.

Troubleshooting

When things seem to be going wrong it can sometimes be owing to something as simple as forgetting to add an ingredient, although at other times it can be harder to work out.

• Did you weigh the ingredients accurately?
• Did you add all the ingredients?
• Did you use the right size pan?
• Have you checked your oven temperature?
• Did you check the cake was properly baked, by testing it?

Frosting and Decorating Cakes

Before frosting or decorating your cake check that it is cold. If not, the frosting will melt off your cake. Also, check that the consistency of your frosting is correct. It needs to be smooth and spreadable.

Storing

Most cakes can be stored in airtight containers for several days. However, cakes made with dairy ingredients, such as cheesecakes, or those with a fresh cream content need to be refrigerated and are best consumed within two days.

Freezing

Most cakes will freeze well. It is best to freeze them unfrosted and undecorated. Make sure they are cold before wrapping them in freezerproof bags. Date and label them clearly. Freeze cakes for up to three months. Defrost overnight at room temperature. However, if they have a high dairy content, such as cheesecakes, defrost overnight in the refrigerator.

. . . .

CHAPTER ONE

Plain Cakes and Loaf Cakes

Buttermilk Cake

A light-tasting, simple cake that's incredibly easy to make.

18 slices

1½ sticks/175g sweet butter, softened
1½ cups/300g sugar
1¼ cups/300ml buttermilk
1 tsp vanilla extract
Scant 2 cups/275g cake flour
1 tsp baking powder
½ tsp baking soda
Pinch salt
4 egg whites

1. Preheat the oven to 350°F/180°C. Grease and base line an 11 x 8 x 1½in/28 x 20 x 4cm baking pan.

2. Cream the butter and sugar together with 1 tbsp of the buttermilk and the vanilla extract.

3. Sift the flour, baking powder, baking soda, and salt together three times. Alternately add the flour and buttermilk to the creamed butter and sugar.

4. In a separate bowl, whisk the egg whites until stiff. Add one-third of the whites to the buttermilk mixture to lighten it, and then fold in the remainder.

5. Pour the batter into the baking pan and bake for 35 to 40 minutes, or until just firm to the touch. Cool in the pan for 5 minutes, then remove onto a wire rack. Cut into slices, to serve.

Brown Sugar Spice Cake

Warming spices richly flavor this easy-to-prepare cake that tastes great served with coffee.

8–10 slices

1½ sticks/175g sweet butter, softened
1¼ cups/250g brown sugar
2 eggs
1⅔ cups/250g all-purpose flour
½ tsp baking powder
1 tsp ground cinnamon
½ tsp freshly grated nutmeg
½ tsp ground ginger
Pinch salt
1 tbsp Demerara sugar

1. Preheat the oven to 350°F/180°C. Grease and base line a 2lb/900g loaf pan.

2. Beat the butter until pale and creamy and then add the brown sugar and beat for another 3 to 4 minutes.

3. Gradually add the eggs and beat well. Sift the flour, baking powder, spices, and salt. Fold into the creamed mixture, adding the milk gradually at the same time.

4. Pour the batter into the prepared pan, sprinkle over the Demerara sugar, and bake for 50 to 55 minutes, or until the cake is firm to the touch and a skewer inserted into the center of the cake comes out clean. Cool in the pan for 5 minutes, then remove onto a wire rack. Cut into slices.

Marble Cake

An impressive cake to serve to friends or family. You can add a chocolate frosting if you prefer (see page 55 for Mississippi Mud Cake frosting).

6–8 slices

Generous 1 cup/175g cake flour
2 tsp baking powder
Pinch salt
⅔ stick/75g sweet butter
1 cup/200g sugar
2 eggs, beaten
½ cup/120ml milk
1 tsp vanilla extract
3oz/75g bittersweet chocolate, melted

1. Preheat the oven to 350°F/180°C. Grease and base line an 8in/20cm round cake pan.

2. Sift the flour, baking powder, and salt and put to one side.

3. Cream the butter and sugar, and gradually add the eggs, a little at a time. Alternately add the flour and milk to the butter mixture and stir in the vanilla extract.

4. Pour half the batter into another bowl and stir in the melted chocolate.

5. Spoon the batters alternately into the prepared pan, and then draw a knife through the mix to create a swirled marble effect. Bake for 35 to 40 minutes, or until the cake is firm to the touch and a skewer inserted into the cake comes out clean.

6. Cool in the pan for 5 minutes, then remove to a wire rack.

Jelly Roll

This homemade sponge cake filled with your favorite jelly is quick and easy to make—ideal for children's parties.

6 slices

⅔ cup/100g cake flour
1½ tsp baking powder
Pinch salt
2 eggs
¾ cup/150g sugar, plus 2 tbsp
½ tsp vanilla extract
2 tbsp 2% milk
6 tbsp strawberry jelly
2 tbsp confectioners' sugar

1. Preheat the oven to 375°F/190°C. Line an 11 x 9in/28 x 23cm jelly roll pan with baking parchment.

2. Sift the flour, baking powder, and salt. Put to one side. Whisk together the eggs and ¾ cup/150g sugar with a hand-held mixer for about 5 minutes, or until thick and creamy. Then stir in the vanilla extract and milk.

3. Fold the dry ingredients into the egg mixture. Pour the batter into the prepared pan and bake for 8 to 10 minutes, or until just firm to the touch.

4. Sprinkle a sheet of baking parchment with the 2 tbsp sugar and turn the sponge out onto it. Wipe over the baking parchment covering the sponge with a clean damp cloth and then peel away the parchment. Roll the sponge up lengthwise and let cool for 10 to 15 minutes.

5. Unroll the sponge, spread with strawberry jelly, and then roll up tightly again. Dust with confectioners' sugar before serving.

Cherry Tea Cake

*Here is a loaf cake that is quick
and simple to make—the perfect cake
to bake in a hurry if unexpected
guests show up.*

8–10 slices

1½ cups/225g all-purpose flour
1 tsp baking powder
2¼ sticks/250g sweet butter, softened
1 cup/200g sugar
3 eggs
3 tbsp 2% milk
1 tsp vanilla extract
½ cup/50g ground almonds
1 cup/150g halved candied cherries

1. Preheat the oven to 350°F/180°C. Grease and base line a 2lb/900g loaf pan.

2. Sift the flour and baking powder together. Cream together the butter and sugar, and beat for 4 to 5minutes, or until pale and fluffy. Gradually beat in the eggs, milk, and vanilla extract. Stir in the flour, ground almonds, and cherries.

3. Spoon the batter into the prepared pan and bake for 50 to 55 minutes, or until firm to the touch or when a skewer inserted into the center of the cake comes out clean. Let cool in the pan for 10 minutes then remove and cool on a wire rack.

Lemon and Poppy Seed Pound Cake

*This poppy seed cake is soaked
with a tangy lemon syrup after it has
been baked to give a superbly moist,
delicious texture. It will keep well
in an airtight container for up to
one week.*

6–8 slices

1½ sticks/175g butter
Scant 1 cup/175g sugar
3 eggs, beaten
Generous 1 cup/175g self-rising flour
1 tbsp poppy seeds
2 tsp grated lemon peel

For the syrup:
3 tbsp sugar
Juice 1 lemon

1. Preheat the oven to 350°F/180°C.
Grease and base line a 2lb/900g loaf pan.

2. Cream the butter and sugar together
until light and fluffy. Gradually beat in the
eggs, a little at a time, and then fold in the
flour, poppy seeds, and lemon peel.

3. Turn the batter into the prepared pan
and bake for 1¼ to 1½ hours, or until risen,
golden, and a skewer inserted into the
center comes out clean. Remove the cake
from the oven but leave in the pan.

4. To make the syrup, gently heat the sugar
and lemon juice together in a pan until the
sugar has dissolved. Bring to a boil then
pour over the cake and let cool. Cut into
slices to serve.

Butter Loaf

Use the best quality ingredients you can for this cake and you'll taste the difference.

8–10 slices

1⅔ cups/250g cake flour
1 tsp baking powder
2¼ sticks/250g sweet butter, softened
1 cup/200g sugar
3 eggs
3 tbsp 2% milk
1 tsp vanilla extract

1. Preheat the oven to 350°F/180°C. Grease and base line a 2lb/900g loaf pan.

2. Sift the flour and baking powder together. Cream together the butter and sugar, and beat for 4 to 5 minutes, or until pale and fluffy. Gradually beat in the eggs, milk, and vanilla extract, and then stir in the flour. Spoon the batter into the prepared pan.

3. Bake for 50 to 55 minutes, or until firm to the touch or when a skewer inserted into the center of the cake comes out clean. Let cool in the pan for 10 minutes then remove and cool on a wire rack.

Simple Raisin Fruit Cake

Allspice and vanilla flavor this sumptuous raisin cake—perfect served with morning coffee.

8–10 slices

1⅔ cups/250g all-purpose flour
1 tsp baking powder
2 sticks/225g sweet butter, softened
1 cup/200g sugar
3 eggs
3 tbsp 2% milk
1 tsp vanilla extract
½ tsp ground allspice
1 cup/200g raisins
1 tbsp confectioners' sugar

1. Preheat the oven to 350°F/180°C. Grease and base line a 2lb/900g loaf pan.

2. Sift the flour and baking powder together. Cream together the butter and sugar. Beat for 4 to 5 minutes, or until pale and fluffy. Gradually beat in the eggs, milk, and vanilla extract. Then stir in the flour, allspice, and raisins.

3. Spoon the batter into the prepared pan and bake for 50 to 55 minutes, or until firm to the touch or when a skewer inserted into the center of the cake comes out clean. Let cool in the pan for 10 minutes, and then remove and cool on a wire rack.

4. Dust lightly with confectioners' sugar before serving.

Pumpkin Spice Cake

Rich and full flavored, this dark, spicy cake is great served with fresh cream.

15 slices

2 cups/300g all-purpose flour
2 tsp baking soda
Pinch salt
3 tsp ground cinnamon
1 tsp freshly grated nutmeg
1½ tsp ground allspice
½ tsp ground ginger
2⅔ sticks/300g butter, softened
1 cup/200g brown sugar
1 cup/200g sugar
2 eggs
1 (15oz/425g) can pumpkin purée
2 cups/200g chopped pecan nuts

1. Preheat the oven to 350°F/180°C. Grease, base line, and flour a 10in/25cm Bundt pan.

2. Sift together the flour, baking soda, salt, and spices and put to one side.

3. Cream together the butter and sugars and, when light and fluffy, gradually add the eggs.

4. Beat in the pumpkin purée and stir in the flour and pecans. Pour the batter into the prepared pan.

5. Bake for 50 to 60 minutes, or until a skewer inserted into the center of the cake comes out clean. Let cool in the pan for 10 minutes then remove and cool on a wire rack.

Cinnamon Swirl Tea Bread

Your reputation as a generous hostess will be greatly enhanced with this rich, spice-scented bread.

10–12 slices

5 cups/750g strong white flour
½ cup/120g granulated sugar
1 tsp salt
2 tbsp active dry yeast
1¼ sticks/125g sweet butter
1¾ cups/400ml milk
2 eggs, beaten
4 heaped tbsp brown sugar
2 tsp ground cinnamon

1. Place the flour, granulated sugar, and salt in a large bowl. Stir in the yeast. Make a well in the center of the flour.

2. Melt the butter in a pan. Pour in the milk and heat until it is just hand hot. Pour the mixture into the well in the flour, add the eggs, and mix together with a wooden spoon until you have a smooth dough.

3. Cover the dough and let rise in a warm place for 45 to 60 minutes, or until it has doubled in size. Mix the brown sugar with the cinnamon.

4. Beat the dough with a wooden spoon to punch down or deflate. With well-floured hands, divide the dough into four pieces. Grease a 10 cup/2.4 liter Kugelhopf mold or two 5 cup/1.2 liter loaf pans.

5. Place a piece of dough in the mold and stretch it around the base until it is covered. Sprinkle over a quarter of the cinnamon sugar mixture. Take a second piece of dough and stretch it over the first one. Sprinkle with cinnamon sugar. Repeat twice more. Let rise for 15 minutes. Meanwhile preheat the oven to 425°F/220°C.

6. Bake for 20 minutes. Reduce the oven temperature to 375°F/190°C and cook the bread for another 5 to 10 minutes. Turn out onto a wire rack and let cool.

Lemon and Ginger Cake

This sharp-tasting, moist cake will keep well—if it lasts that long!

8–10 slices

1⅔ cups/250g all-purpose flour
1 tsp baking powder
2¼ sticks/250g sweet butter, softened
1 cup/200g sugar
3 eggs
3 tbsp 2% milk
½ cup/50g ground almonds
1 tsp ground ginger
2 tbsp grated lemon peel
2 tbsp finely shredded candied
   lemon peel

1. Preheat the oven to 350°F/180°C. Grease and base line a 2lb/900g loaf pan.

2. Sift the flour and baking powder together. Cream the butter and sugar. Beat for 4 to 5 minutes, or until pale and fluffy. Gradually beat in the eggs and milk, and stir in the flour, ground almonds, ginger, and lemon peel.

3. Spoon the batter into the prepared pan and bake for 55 to 60 minutes, or until firm to the touch or when a skewer inserted into the center of the cake comes out clean. Let cool in the pan for 10 minutes, then remove and cool on a wire rack.

4. Spread the candied lemon peel over the top of the cake before serving.

Cook's Tip:
Make your own candied peel. Bring strips of unwaxed lemon peel from 2 lemons to a boil. Drain and refresh under cold water. Repeat this process. Finely shred the peel. Return to the pan with enough water to cover and ½ cup/100g sugar. Dissolve the sugar and simmer until the syrup thickens. Cool slightly. Spoon the peel over the top of the cake.

Molasses Gingerbread

Everyone will enjoy this afternoon treat—it's really a hybrid of a cake and a teabread and is delicious served with sweet butter.

8–10 slices

2⅔ cups/400g all-purpose flour
1 tsp baking powder
1 tbsp ground ginger
1 tsp ground cinnamon
2 sticks/225g sweet butter
½ cup/125g dark molasses
¾ cup/175g brown sugar
3 eggs
3oz/75g candied cherries, halved
4oz/115g chopped dried dates
2oz/55g preserved ginger
¾ cup/90g golden raisins

1. Grease and line an 8½in/22cm square cake pan, and preheat the oven to 300°F/150°C.

2. Mix together the flour, baking powder, ground ginger, and cinnamon in a large bowl.

3. Place the butter in a pan with the molasses and brown sugar, and stir over low heat until melted. Pour it into the flour mixture and mix well. Beat in the eggs and stir in the remaining ingredients.

4. Pour the batter into the prepared cake pan and bake for 1 to 1¼ hours, or until a skewer inserted into the center comes out clean. Turn out onto a wire rack and let cool.

Caribbean Banana Bread

A great way to use up overripe bananas that no one wants to eat—they are transformed into a moist and spicy cake.

6–8 slices

2 bananas, peeled
2 tbsp clear honey
1½ cups/200g self-rising flour
½ tsp baking powder
1 tsp freshly grated nutmeg
1⅓ sticks/150g butter, softened
¾ cup/175g packed light brown sugar
2 eggs, beaten
⅓ cup/50g pecan nuts, finely chopped

1. Preheat the oven to 350°F/180°C. Grease an 8 x 4 x 3in/20 x 10 x 7.5cm loaf pan and base line with baking parchment.

2. Mash the bananas with the honey. Sift the flour, baking powder, and nutmeg together in a separate bowl.

3. Cream the butter and sugar in a large mixing bowl until light and fluffy. Gradually add the eggs beating well between additions.

4. Fold in the bananas and the flour mixture with the pecans. Spoon the batter into the prepared loaf pan. Bake for 50 minutes to 1 hour, or until golden and a skewer inserted into the center comes out clean.

5. Let cool in the pan for 10 minutes before turning out onto a wire rack to cool completely.

CHAPTER TWO

Coffee Cakes

Yeasted Sour Cream Cake

8–10 slices

1 tsp active dry yeast
2 cups/300g all-purpose flour
⅓ cup/75g sour cream
⅓ cup/75g cream cheese
1⅓ sticks/150g sweet butter, melted
½ cup/100g sugar
2 eggs
2 egg yolks
1 tsp ground cinnamon
4 tbsp slivered almonds
3 tbsp apricot jelly
3 tbsp confectioners' sugar
1 tbsp lemon juice

1. Grease a 2lb/900g loaf pan. Dissolve the yeast in ½ cup/120ml of warm water and add 2 tbsp flour. Stand in a warm place until the yeast starts to froth (about 10 minutes).

2. Mix together the sour cream, cream cheese, and melted butter. Then add the sugar, eggs, and yolks and put to one side.

3. When the yeast has started to work add the remaining flour and cinnamon to the yeast mixture and stir in. Add the sour cream mixture and work to form a soft dough. Cover with a clean damp cloth and prove for 1 hour in a warm place until doubled in size.

4. Mix in the almonds then pour the dough into the pan. Let the dough rise again for 20 to 30 minutes. Meanwhile, preheat the oven to 375°F/190°C.

5. Bake for 25 to 30 minutes, or until golden. Remove from the pan and place on a wire rack, to cool completely.

6. Gently heat the apricot jelly with 3 tbsp of water and brush over the top of the cake. Mix the confectioner's sugar with 1 tbsp lemon juice and drizzle over the cake.

Coffee, Maple, and Pecan Sponge Cake

6–8 slices

½ cup/75g all-purpose flour
Pinch salt
3 tbsp/40g sweet butter
3 large eggs
6 tbsp/75g sugar
1 tsp instant coffee powder
½ tsp vanilla extract

For the frosting:
1½ sticks/175g butter
Scant 1 cup/100g confectioners' sugar
1 tsp instant coffee powder
4 tbsp maple syrup
8 pecan nut halves, to decorate

1. Preheat the oven to 350°C/180°C. Grease and line an 8in/20cm round cake pan. Sift the flour and salt together three times and set aside. Melt the butter.

2. Break the eggs into a large bowl and add the sugar. Set over a pan of simmering water and beat with a hand-held mixer until thick and frothy and the beaters leave a trail when lifted out of the mixture.

3. Dissolve the coffee in 1 tbsp hot water, then beat into the eggs with the vanilla. Sift the flour over the eggs in three batches, drizzling a little butter around the bowl in between each batch and folding in.

4. Pour into the pan and bake for 25 to 30 minutes, or until golden. Cool in the pan for 2 to 3 minutes, then turn out onto a wire rack to cool completely.

5. For the frosting, beat the butter and sugar together until smooth. Dissolve the coffee in 1 tbsp hot water, and then gradually beat this into the frosting with the maple syrup until smooth.

6. Cut the cake twice horizontally to make three layers, and spread the frosting over each layer. Assemble the cake and spread the remaining frosting around the sides and top. Decorate with pecans.

Passion Cake

A thick, indulgent layer of sweet, cream cheese frosting makes this cake extra special. Walnuts can be substituted for the pecans.

6–8 slices

⅔ cup/160ml safflower oil
¾ cup/175g packed light brown sugar
3 eggs, beaten
½ tsp ground cinnamon
½ tsp freshly grated nutmeg
5oz/150g carrots, coarsely grated
1 banana, mashed
⅓ cup/50g pecan nuts, chopped
1⅔ cups/250g all-purpose flour, sifted
1 tbsp baking powder

For the frosting:
⅔ cup/160g cream cheese, softened
Scant 1 cup/100g confectioners'
    sugar, sifted
Grated peel of ½ orange
½ cup/50g chopped pecan nuts
    (optional)

1. Preheat the oven to 350°F/180°C. Grease and base line an 8in/20cm square cake pan.

2. Put all the cake ingredients into a large mixing bowl and beat together well.

3. Spoon the batter into the prepared pan and spread evenly. Bake for 45 to 50 minutes, or until golden and a skewer inserted into the center comes out clean.

4. Let cool in the pan for 10 minutes, then turn out onto a wire rack to cool completely.

5. To make the frosting, beat the cream cheese, sugar, and orange peel together until light and fluffy. Spread over the top of the cake and sprinkle with pecans before serving, if liked.

Blueberry Coffee Cake with Streusel Topping

Soft blueberries, a creamy cheese filling, and a crunchy topping make this cake an unusual treat.

8–10 slices

4 cups/600g all-purpose flour
4 tsp baking powder
1 tsp salt
1¼ sticks/125g butter, softened
1¼ cups/250g sugar
2 eggs, lightly beaten
1½ tsp vanilla extract
1¼ cups/300ml milk
3 cups/350g fresh blueberries

For the topping:
⅔ cup/130g sugar
⅓ cup/65g packed light brown sugar
1¼ sticks/125g butter, softened
⅔ cup/100g all-purpose flour
½ cup/50g chopped, toasted walnuts or
    pecan nuts
1½ tsp ground cinnamon
½ tsp freshly grated nutmeg
½ tsp salt

For the filling:
12oz/350g cream cheese, softened
⅓ cup/65g sugar
1 egg
Grated peel of 1 lemon
1–2 tbsp fresh lemon juice
1 tsp vanilla extract

1. Preheat the oven to 375°F/190°C and generously grease a 13 x 9in/33 x 23cm glass baking dish.

2. To make the topping, rub together the sugars, butter, and flour in a bowl, until the mixture forms large crumbs. Stir in the nuts, cinnamon, nutmeg, and salt. Refrigerate until ready to use.

3. To make the filling, beat the cream cheese in a bowl using an electric mixer, until creamy. Gradually beat in the sugar. Beat in the egg, lemon peel, juice, and vanilla extract. Set aside.

4. Sift the flour, baking powder, and salt into a bowl. In a clean bowl, beat the butter with an electric mixer, until creamy. Gradually beat in the sugar until the mixture is fluffy. Then beat in the eggs and vanilla extract. On low speed, beat in the flour alternately with the milk to blend well. Fold in the blueberries.

5. Spread a little less than half the cake batter onto the base of the dish. Gently spread the filling evenly over the cake batter, and then sprinkle a quarter of the topping over the filling. Drop spoonfuls of the remaining cake batter over the top and spread evenly. Sprinkle the remaining topping over the surface.

6. Bake for about 1 hour, or until crunchy and golden on top. Remove to a wire rack and cool. Cut into squares, and serve warm or at room temperature.

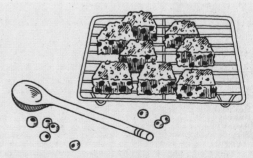

Coconut Cake

You can enjoy this moist and tasty cake at any time of day. It's also useful to add to kids' lunch boxes.

6–8 slices

1¼ sticks/125g sweet butter, softened
¾ cup/150g sugar
1 cup/240ml buttermilk
1 tsp vanilla extract
1⅓ cups/200g all-purpose flour
1 tsp baking powder
½ tsp baking soda
Pinch salt
1 cup/100g flaked coconut
4 egg whites

1. Preheat the oven to 350°F/180°C. Grease and base line a 9in/23cm round cake pan.

2. Cream together the butter and sugar, and then mix in the buttermilk and vanilla extract. Sift together the flour, baking powder, baking soda, and salt, and then stir into the butter mixture. Add the coconut, less 2 tbsp, and combine well.

3. Beat the egg whites stiffly and then add one-third to the cake mixture. Stir in to lighten the mix then fold in the remainder. Pour the batter into the pan, and sprinkle with the reserved 2 tbsp coconut. Bake for 30 to 35 minutes, or until firm to the touch and golden in color. Remove from the pan and let cool.

Orange and Almond Sponge Cake

This moist sponge cake is a great accompaniment to morning coffee and is special enough for dessert, too.

6–8 slices

1½ sticks/175g butter
Scant 1 cup/175g sugar
3 eggs
1 cup/150g self-rising flour
½ cup/50g ground almonds
Few drops almond extract

For the frosting:
1¼ (8oz/225g) packages cream cheese
2 tbsp fresh orange juice
2 tsp grated orange peel
Scant 1 cup/100g confectioners'
   sugar, sifted
Toasted slivered almonds and shredded
   orange peel, to decorate

1. Preheat the oven to 375°F/190°C. Grease and line the bases of two 8in/20cm round sandwich pans.

2. Beat the butter and sugar with a hand-held mixer in a bowl until pale and fluffy.

3. Beat the eggs, and then gradually beat into the butter and sugar mixture. Sift the flour and almonds over the top and add the almond extract. Fold into the mixture gently until combined.

4. Spoon the batter into the pans and level the surfaces. Bake for 20 to 25 minutes, or until golden and the centers of the cakes spring back when lightly pressed.

5. Turn out of the pans and cool on a wire rack. Meanwhile, make the frosting. Beat the cream cheese in a bowl to soften. Add the orange juice, orange peel, and sugar, and beat until smooth and creamy.

6. Sandwich the cakes together with a little frosting, and spread the rest of the frosting over the top. Scatter toasted, sliced almonds and orange peel over to decorate.

Yeasted Pecan Cake

8 slices

2 tsp active dry yeast
2 cups/300g all-purpose flour
¾ cup/150g sugar
2 tsp ground cinnamon
3 eggs
⅔ cup/160ml vegetable oil
½ cup/75g golden raisins
1 cup/100g chopped pecan nuts
½ stick/50g cold sweet butter,
  cut into pieces
1 cup/100g pecan nuts, ground in a
  food processor
3 tbsp 2% milk
½ cup/55g confectioners' sugar

1. Preheat the oven to 375°F/190°C. Grease a 9in/23cm round cake pan. Dissolve the yeast in ½ cup/120ml of warm water and add ½ cup/75g flour and 1 tsp sugar. Set in a warm place until the yeast starts to work (about 10 minutes).

2. Add the remaining flour in a large bowl, less 3 tbsp for the topping. Stir in half the cinnamon and ½ cup/100g of the sugar, and pour in the yeast mixture. Mix well. Cover the dough with a clean damp cloth and let rise for 30 minutes in a warm place.

3. Stir in the eggs and oil and work to form a smooth dough. Mix in the golden raisins and chopped pecans. Press the dough into the pan and prove for 40 to 45 minutes.

4. Rub together the remaining sugar, the reserved 3 tbsp flour, half the butter, the remaining cinnamon, and the ground pecans until the mixture starts to clump together. Sprinkle over the dough.

5. Bake for 25 to 30 minutes, or until golden. Remove from the pan and place on a wire rack. Heat the milk and add the remaining butter. When melted stir in the confectioners' sugar and pour over the warm cake. Serve warm.

Apple Crumb Cake

A great balance of flavors and textures make this a fantastic cake.

6-8 slices

1 stick plus 3 tbsp/140g sweet butter
1lb/450g sharp-tasting apples, peeled,
   cored, and chopped
1 tsp ground cinnamon
½ tsp freshly grated nutmeg
1½ cups/225g all-purpose flour
¾ cup/150g sugar
2 eggs
3 tbsp sour cream
1 tsp vanilla extract
½ tsp baking powder
¼ tsp baking soda
Pinch salt

1. Preheat the oven to 350°F/180°C. Grease and base line an 8in/20cm round cake pan.

2. Melt 2 tbsp butter in a small pan and add the apples, sprinkle in half the cinnamon and the nutmeg, and stir to coat the apples in the butter. Place a disk of baking parchment on top of the apples, reduce the heat, and cook gently for 5 to 10 minutes, stirring, until the apples are tender.

3. Rub together 4 tbsp flour, 2 tbsp butter, and 2 tbsp sugar, until the mixture forms large clumps. Set this crumb topping aside.

4. Cream together the remaining butter and sugar, and gradually beat in the eggs. Beat in the sour cream and vanilla extract.

5. Sift together the remaining flour and cinnamon, the baking powder, baking soda, and salt. Stir the dry ingredients into the butter mixture.

6. Stir in the warm apples, and pour the batter into the prepared pan. Sprinkle over the crumb topping and bake for 40 to 45 minutes, or until golden or when a skewer inserted into the center of the cake comes out clean. Let cool and serve.

Herman Coffee Cake

You will need to make and "feed" a "starter" for this cake, which takes 15 days to grow. The starter gives the cake its distinctive flavor.

15 slices

1½ cups/300g sugar
2 cups/300g all-purpose flour
½ tsp salt
2 tsp ground cinnamon
½ tsp baking soda
2 tsp baking powder
⅔ cup/160ml vegetable oil
2 eggs
1 cup/100g chopped pecan nuts
¾ cup/150g raisins
4 tbsp margarine
2 tbsp milk
Scant 1 cup/100g confectioners' sugar

For the starter:
2¼ tsp active dry yeast
2 cups/480ml warm water

1¼ cups/200g all-purpose flour
¼ cup/50g sugar

For the feed:
½ cup/100g sugar
1 cup/150g all-purpose flour
1 cup/240ml milk

1. For the starter, dissolve the yeast in the warm water and stir in the flour and sugar with a wooden spoon (do not use a metal spoon).

2. Cover and store in a warm place overnight. The next day, stir and refrigerate. Stir once a day for the first four days. On the fifth day stir then divide in half. Either discard one half or give it away with feeding instructions.

3. Feed the starter on the fifth day, as follows: add half the sugar, half the flour, and half the milk. Cover and refrigerate. Stir once a day for the next four days, then feed again as before on the tenth day. Cover and refrigerate. Stir once a day for the next four days.

4. On the fifteenth day the starter is ready to use. Reserve 1 cup in the refrigerator and continue to follow the feed cycle, if you want to make another cake.

5. Preheat the oven to 350°F/180°C. Grease a 9 x 13 x 1½in/23 x 33 x 4cm deep pan.

6. Mix together 2 cups of the starter, 1 cup of the sugar, and the flour, less 3 tbsp. Add the salt, half the cinnamon, the baking soda, baking powder, oil, and eggs. Stir to combine. Stir in the pecans and the raisins and pour into the prepared pan.

7. Using your fingertips, rub together ½ cup sugar, the 3 tbsp flour, half the margarine and the remaining cinnamon until they start to clump together. Then sprinkle this topping over the dough.

8. Bake for 20 to 25 minutes. To make the glaze, heat the milk and add the remaining margarine. When it has melted add the confectioners' sugar. Remove the cake from the oven and pour over the glaze while still warm.

Yellow Cake with Creamy Frosting

An almond and raisin topping completes this light, moist sponge.

8 slices

2¼ sticks/250g sweet butter
1½ cups/300g sugar
3 eggs
5 egg yolks
1⅓ cups/200g cake flour
1 tsp baking powder
¾ cup/180ml milk

For the frosting:
4 egg whites
½ cup/100g sugar
Pinch cream of tartar
2 tbsp golden raisins
2 tbsp slivered almonds

1. Preheat the oven to 350°F/180°C. Grease and base line a 9in/23cm round cake pan.

2. Cream together the butter and sugar until light and fluffy. Gradually add the eggs and egg yolks, beating well between each addition. Fold in the flour and baking powder alternately with the milk.

3. Spoon into the prepared pan. Bake the cake for 30 to 35 minutes. When golden and firm to the touch remove from the oven.

4. To make the frosting, beat the egg whites and gradually add the sugar, whisking until stiff peaks form. Add the cream of tartar. Spread the frosting over the cake and sprinkle with the fruit and nuts. Return to the oven for 4 to 5 minutes to give the frosting a little color. Remove and let cool.

CHAPTER THREE

....

Chocolate Cakes

Chocolate Fudge Layer Cake

A dreamy cake for true chocolate lovers everywhere.

8 slices

9oz/250g bittersweet chocolate, chopped
1½ sticks/175g sweet butter
¾ cup/175g packed soft brown sugar
4 eggs, beaten
1 cup/150g all-purpose flour
1 tsp baking powder
¾ cup/75g finely ground almonds

For the filling:
½ cup/75g unsweetened cocoa powder
¾ cup/175g packed soft brown sugar
Scant ½ cup/50g confectioners' sugar
1½ sticks/175g sweet butter, melted

For the frosting:
5oz/150g semisweet chocolate
½ stick/50g sweet butter
1oz/25g bittersweet chocolate, melted (optional)

1. Preheat the oven to 350°F/180°C. Grease and line two 8in/20cm cake pans. Melt the chocolate with 4 tbsp water in a bowl set over a pan of gently simmering water. Let cool slightly.

2. Cream the butter and sugar together until light and fluffy. Gradually add the eggs. Stir in the melted chocolate, then fold in the flour, baking powder, and almonds. Pour into pans.

3. Bake for 20 to 25 minutes. Let cool slightly, then invert the cakes on a wire rack. Slice each cake through the center, to make four layers.

4. To make the filling, mix together the cocoa and sugars. Beat in the melted butter and stir in 4 tbsp boiling water to form a smooth paste. Refrigerate for 20 minutes, then spread evenly over three layers of the cake. Place the final cake layer on top.

5. To make the frosting, melt the semisweet chocolate and butter in a bowl over a pan of simmering water. Beat until glossy, then let cool to a spreading consistency. Smooth evenly over the top of the cake.

German Chocolate Cake

*A rich, buttery, nutty frosting works
well with this light chocolate sponge.*

8–10 slices

4oz/115g bittersweet chocolate
1½ sticks/175g sweet butter
1½ cups/300g sugar
3 eggs
1⅓ cups/200g cake flour
1 tsp baking soda
Pinch salt
1 cup/240ml buttermilk

For the filling:
1½ cups/350ml evaporated milk
1½ cups/300g sugar
1½ sticks/175g sweet butter
4 egg yolks
2 tsp vanilla extract
7oz/200g sweetened flaked coconut
1½ cups/150g chopped pecan nuts

1. Preheat the oven to 350°F/180°C. Grease
and base line three 8in/20cm round pans.

2. Melt the chocolate and butter in a large
bowl over a pan of gently simmering water.
Stir to melt the chocolate and then stir in
the sugar. Beat in the eggs gradually on a
low speed using a hand-held mixer.

3. Beat in ⅓ cup/50g of the flour, the
baking soda, and salt. Add the remaining
flour alternately with the buttermilk. Beat
well for 1 minute to give a smooth batter.

4. Divide the batter between the pans and
bake for 25 to 30 minutes. Let cool on a
wire rack.

5. To make the filling, pour the evaporated
milk into a pan and add the sugar, butter,
egg yolks, and vanilla extract. Cook over
medium heat, stirring constantly, for 10 to
12 minutes. The mixture will thicken and
turn golden brown. Remove from the heat,
strain, and then stir in the coconut and
pecans. Cool to room temperature before
using to fill and cover the sponges.

Chocolate and Strawberry Layer Cake

A dark chocolate frosting perfectly complements the sweet fruit filling in this luxurious chocolate cake.

8–10 slices

9oz/250g bittersweet chocolate, chopped
¾ cup/180ml milk
2¼ sticks/250g sweet butter
1 cup/225g packed dark brown sugar
3 eggs
1⅓ cups/200g cake flour
1 tbsp baking powder
4 tbsp unsweetened cocoa powder
4 tbsp strawberry compote or jelly
Scant ½ cup/50g confectioners' sugar

1. Preheat the oven to 325°F/160°C. Grease and base line two 8in/20cm round cake pans.

2. Melt 3½oz/100g of the chocolate and the milk together in a heatproof bowl set over a pan of simmering water.

3. Using a hand-held mixer, cream together 1¼ sticks/125g butter and 1 cup/225g sugar until light and fluffy, and then gradually add the eggs.

4. Sift the flour, baking powder, and cocoa together and add alternately with the chocolate milk to the butter mix. Increase the speed for about 30 seconds to mix the batter thoroughly.

5. Divide the batter between the pans and bake for 25 to 30 minutes, or until firm to the touch. Let cool before filling.

6. Melt and cool the remaining chocolate. Sandwich the two layers together with the strawberry compote or jelly. Cream the remaining butter in a bowl, and add the confectioners' sugar. Pour in the melted, cooled chocolate and mix well. Spread the cake with the frosting and serve with whipped cream, if liked.

Devil's Food Cake with Chocolate-Orange Frosting

This is a real chocoholic's delight: wickedly indulgent, rich, and sweet.

8 slices

6oz/175g bittersweet chocolate
1⅓ sticks/150g sweet butter
½ cup/100g sugar
6 large eggs, separated
½ cup/75g all-purpose flour
⅔ cup/50g ground almonds

For the frosting:
Generous ¾ cup/200ml whipping cream
7oz/200g bittersweet chocolate
2 tsp grated orange peel
Confectioners' sugar, for dusting

1. Preheat the oven to 350°F/180°C. Grease and line an 8in/20cm round cake pan with baking parchment.

2. Melt the chocolate in a bowl over a pan of gently simmering water. Cool slightly.

3. Beat the butter and half the sugar until creamy. Beat in the melted chocolate then the egg yolks, one at a time.

4. Sift the flour and almonds together into a separate bowl. Beat the egg whites in a separate bowl until stiff, and then gradually beat in the remaining sugar. Stir half the egg whites into the chocolate mixture to loosen it slightly, and then fold in the flour and almond mix with the remaining egg white.

5. Spoon into the pan and bake for 50 to 60 minutes, or until a skewer inserted into the center comes out clean. Cool in the pan for 10 minutes. Remove from the pan and leave until cold.

6. To make the frosting, heat the cream in a pan until nearly boiling. Remove from the heat and stir in the chocolate until melted, then stir in the orange peel. Keep stirring until thick. Spread evenly over the top and sides of the cake. Let set before dusting with confectioners' sugar.

Mississippi Mud Cake

Top quality chocolate will bring out the best in this rich and tempting chocolate and nut extravaganza.

8–10 slices

2¼ sticks/250g butter
1¼ cups/250g sugar
3 eggs
4oz/115g bittersweet chocolate, melted
1 tsp vanilla extract
1½ cups/225g all-purpose flour
4 tbsp unsweetened cocoa powder
½ tsp baking powder
Pinch salt
1 cup/100g chopped pecan nuts

For the frosting:
1¼ sticks/125g sweet butter
½ cup/55g confectioners' sugar
5oz/150g bittersweet chocolate, melted
Unsweetened cocoa powder and
    confectioners' sugar, for dredging

1. Preheat the oven to 350°F/180°C. Grease a 9in/23cm Bundt pan.

2. Cream together the butter and sugar, and gradually beat in the eggs. Add the melted chocolate and vanilla extract.

3. Sift the flour, cocoa powder, baking powder, and salt together and stir into the chocolate mixture. Stir in the pecans. Spoon into the prepared pan, and bake for 40 to 45 minutes, or when a skewer inserted into the center of the cake comes out clean. Remove from the oven and let cool in the pan for 10 minutes. Remove and leave until cold.

4. To make the frosting, beat the butter until pale and fluffy. Beat in the confectioners' sugar and then stir in the melted chocolate. Place the cake on a plate, flat base uppermost, and spread with the chocolate frosting. Dredge with cocoa powder and a little confectioners' sugar before serving.

Black Cherry and Chocolate Cake

*Enter this on the food roll of honor.
The classic Black Forest Gâteau.*

12 slices

2 (15oz/425g) cans pitted black cherries
1 cup/120ml rum
6 eggs
1 cup/200g sugar
1 cup/150g cake flour
5 tbsp unsweetened cocoa powder
600ml/1pt heavy whipping cream
3 tbsp black cherry jelly
4oz/115g bittersweet chocolate

1. Preheat the oven to 400°F/200°C. Grease and base line two 9in/23cm round cake pans. Put the cherries in a bowl and pour over half the rum.

2. Put the eggs and sugar, less 3 tbsp in a large mixing bowl over a pan of simmering water and beat with a hand-held mixer for 15 to 20 minutes until the mixture is thick, pale, and holds its own weight. Sift the flour and cocoa powder together. Remove the eggs from the heat and fold in the flour and cocoa powder.

3. Pour the mix into the prepared pans and bake for 12 to 15 minutes. Remove from the pans and cool on a wire rack.

4. Lightly beat the cream and stir in the rum and remaining sugar.

5. When the cake is cool brush each of the sponge layers with some of the rum that the cherries have been soaking in and then spread the jelly over one of the sponges. Top this sponge with one third of the cream and the cherries, reserving 12 for decoration. Place the other layer of sponge on top and cover the sides and top of the cake with cream, reserving some to decorate. Cover the cake with the grated chocolate and pipe 12 rosettes of cream around the edge of the cake. Top with the reserved cherries.

6. Refrigerate for 45 minutes before serving.

Chocolate and Chestnut Macaroon Cake

Drizzle each slice of this cake with melted dark chocolate before serving.

6–8 slices

Scant 2¼ cups/300g confectioners' sugar
½ tsp baking soda
4 large egg whites
Generous 2 cups/200g ground almonds

For the filling:
Scant ½ cup/100g chestnut purée
2 tbsp maple syrup
3oz/75g bittersweet chocolate
2½ cups/250g mascarpone cheese
Scant ⅔ cup/150ml whipping cream
Chocolate curls, to decorate

1. Preheat the oven to 275°F/140°C. Line three baking sheets with baking parchment and draw a 7in/18cm circle on each.

2. Sift the confectioners' sugar and baking soda together. Beat the egg whites until stiff. Gradually beat in three-quarters of the confectioners' sugar until stiff and glossy. Mix the rest into the ground almonds then fold into the whites. Divide the mixture between the three circles and spread out evenly.

3. Bake for 10 minutes. Reduce the oven temperature to 225°F/110°C and cook for another 1¼ hours. Cool on a wire rack and then peel away the parchment.

4. To make the filling, beat the chestnut purée and maple syrup together until smooth. Melt the chocolate in a bowl set over a pan of hot water. Stir the melted chocolate into the chestnut purée, and then beat in the mascarpone cheese followed by the cream.

5. Place a meringue circle on a serving plate and spread with half the chestnut mixture. Place a second meringue circle on top and spread that carefully with the remaining chestnut mixture. Top with the remaining meringue and decorate with chocolate curls.

Cappuccino Truffle Cake

*This coffee and chocolate combo is
more like a cold soufflé than a cake.*

6–8 slices

1 tbsp instant coffee powder
Scant ⅔ cup/150ml boiling water
½ cup/100g no-need-to-soak pitted
  prunes, chopped
4 tbsp Tia Maria, or other coffee liqueur
6oz/175g bittersweet chocolate
1 stick/115g butter, plus extra for
  greasing
5 eggs, separated
½ cup/100g sugar
1 tsp vanilla extract
1 tbsp cornstarch
Unsweetened cocoa powder, for dusting
Whipped cream, to serve

1. Dissolve the coffee powder in the boiling
water, then pour over the prunes in a bowl
with the Tia Maria. Let soak overnight.

2. Preheat the oven to 325°F/160°C. Grease
and line a deep 8in/20cm springform cake
pan with baking parchment.

3. Melt the chocolate and butter together in
a bowl set over a pan of hot water. Beat the
egg yolks and sugar with a hand-held mixer
until they are thick and frothy and the beaters
leave a trail when lifted out of the mixture.
Stir in the vanilla extract, prunes, and melted
chocolate mixtures and set aside.

4. With clean beaters, beat the egg whites in
a bowl until stiff. Beat in the cornstarch and
fold into the chocolate mixture. Pour into the
prepared pan and bake for 50 minutes, or
until springy to the touch. Let cool in the pan.

5. Dust with cocoa powder. Cut into slices
and serve topped with whipped cream.

Peppermint Chocolate Layer Cake

Crunchy peppermints top this minty, frosted chocolate cake—a surefire favorite with kids.

10–12 slices

6oz/175g bittersweet chocolate
⅔ stick/75g sweet butter
2½ cups/500g sugar
3 egg yolks
1½ cups/350ml milk
2 cups/300g cake flour
Pinch salt
¼ tsp baking soda
2 tsp vanilla extract

For the frosting:
3 egg whites
2 cups/400g sugar
Pinch salt
¼ tsp cream of tartar
3 tbsp water
2–3 drops pale green food coloring
2–3 drops peppermint extract
¼ cup/50g crushed peppermint candies

1. Preheat the oven to 350°F/180°C. Grease and base line three 8in/20cm round pans.

2. Melt the chocolate and butter in a large bowl set over a pan of gently simmering water, then let cool to room temperature. Stir in the sugar. Add the egg yolks and half the milk, and mix well.

3. Add the flour, salt, and soda and beat for 1 minute with an electric mixer. Blend in the remaining milk and the vanilla extract, and pour into the prepared pans.

4. Bake for 25 to 30 minutes, or until just firm to the touch. Cool on a wire rack.

5. To make the frosting, mix the egg whites, sugar, salt, cream of tartar, and water in a bowl set over a pan of gently simmering water. Cook over boiling water for 7 minutes, beating until the frosting forms firm peaks. Remove from the heat and add the food coloring and peppermint extract. Use to fill and top the cake. Decorate with the crushed candies.

Chocolate Refrigerator Cake

Refrigerator cakes are always a great favorite with adults and kids alike. This one is simple and quick to make and you can substitute any preferred fruits, if you like.

12–15 slices

1lb/450g bittersweet chocolate
2¼ sticks/250g sweet butter
12oz/350g broken shortbread cookies or
   Graham crackers
2 cups/200g chopped pecan nuts
1 cup/150g raisins
1 cup/150g halved red candied cherries

1. Grease and line a 2lb/900g loaf pan with a double layer of plastic wrap.

2. Melt the chocolate and butter in a large mixing bowl set over a pan of gently simmering water. Remove the bowl. Add the remaining ingredients and stir to ensure the ingredients are well mixed.

3. Spoon the mixture into the lined pan, cover, and refrigerate for 2 to 3 hours or until firm enough to turn out and slice.

Variations:
- You can substitute ginger cookies or any other favorite for those used in the recipe.
- Add a handful of mini-marshmallows, if liked.

CHAPTER FOUR

Cheesecakes

Cheesecake Deluxe

Popular in the 1950s, this recipe has stood the test of time because it's so tasty!

8 slices

1½ cups/100g fine Graham
    cracker crumbs
3 tbsp sugar
1 tsp ground cinnamon
½ tsp freshly grated nutmeg
⅔ stick/75g butter

For the filling:
½ stick/50g butter
½ cup/100g sugar
Pinch salt
1 tbsp grated lemon peel
3 large eggs, separated
Juice 1 lemon
½ tsp vanilla extract
2 (8oz/225g) packages cream cheese
1 cup/240ml sour cream

1. Preheat the oven to 300°F/150°C. Combine the Graham cracker crumbs with the sugar, cinnamon, and nutmeg. Melt the butter, blend it into the crumb mixture, and pack firmly against the base and sides of a 9in/23cm springform cake pan or ovenproof glass dish. Place in the refrigerator to chill.

2. To make the filling, cream together the butter, sugar, salt, and lemon peel. Slowly beat the egg yolks into the creamed mixture. Add the lemon juice, vanilla extract, cream cheese, and sour cream. Beat the egg whites until soft peaks form. Fold into the other ingredients and ladle onto the base.

3. Bake the cheesecake for 1 to 1¼ hours, or until firm. Let cool in the pan, and then remove the springform sides. Slide the cheesecake off the pan's base and onto a serving plate. Refrigerate for several hours before serving.

Strawberry Cheesecake

Serve this cheesecake with its glorious topping of strawberries and purée.

10–12 slices

3 cups/225g Graham crackers, finely
  crushed
½ stick/50g butter, melted
¼ cup/50g candied peel, very finely
  chopped (optional)

For the filling:
2¼ cups/600g whole cream cheese
¾ cup/175g granulated sugar
1 tsp vanilla extract
1¼ cups/300ml whipping cream,
  whipped to soft peaks

For the topping:
4 cups/500g strawberries, hulled
2–3 tbsp confectioners' sugar, to taste
Juice ½ lemon

1. Lightly oil an 8in/20cm springform cake pan. Mix the cracker crumbs with the melted butter and candied peel, if using. Spread in an even layer over the base of the pan and press down well. Refrigerate.

2. For the filling, beat together the cheese, sugar, and vanilla extract until smooth. Carefully fold in the cream. Spread this mixture evenly on top of the chilled base and refrigerate for at least 4 hours, preferably overnight.

3. For the topping, put 1 cup/150g of the strawberries into a food processor with the confectioners' sugar and lemon juice. Blend to a purée. Strain to remove the seeds, then halve the remaining strawberries and put into a bowl with the puréed strawberries and mix. Taste and add more sugar if necessary.

4. To serve, remove the cake from the pan and transfer to a serving plate. Spoon the purée over the top, letting a little run down the sides. Top with the remaining strawberries and serve.

New York Cheesecake

You can dress up or dress down this American classic. Serve plain or topped with fruit compote.

12–15 slices

7oz/200g Graham cracker crumbs
½ stick/50g sweet butter, melted
4 (8oz/225g) packages cream cheese
Pinch salt
1½ cups/300g sugar
1 cup/240ml sour cream
2 tsp vanilla extract
1 tbsp lemon peel
1 tbsp lemon juice
4 eggs
2 egg yolks

1. Preheat the oven to 300°F/150°C. Grease a 9in/23cm springform cake pan.

2. Mix together the Graham cracker crumbs and melted butter and press into the base of the pan. Bake for 10 minutes, or until lightly browned, and then let cool.

3. Beat the cream cheese until soft and smooth. Add the salt and sugar, and beat for 1 minute.

4. Add the sour cream, vanilla extract, lemon peel, and juice, and beat for another minute. Add the eggs and yolks, and beat to combine. Pour the mixture onto the cooled base.

5. Bake for 45 to 50 minutes, or until the edges are set but the center is still slightly soft. Turn off the oven, leave the cheesecake inside, and leave the door ajar. Let cool in the oven for 45 minutes.

6. Remove the cheesecake and cool to room temperature. Remove from the pan, cover with foil, and refrigerate for at least 4 hours, preferably overnight, before serving.

Whipped Cream Cheesecake

An exceptionally light and creamy cheesecake that makes a flamboyant centerpiece at a dinner party.

12–15 slices

7oz/200g Graham cracker crumbs
4 tbsp sweet butter, melted
3 (8oz/225g) packages cream cheese
Pinch salt
3 tbsp cornstarch
1 cup/200g sugar
2 eggs
2 egg yolks
2 tsp vanilla extract
1 tsp vanilla seeds (optional)
2½ cups/600ml heavy whipping cream
Fruit, to decorate

1. Preheat the oven to 300°F/150°C. Grease a 9in/23cm springform cake pan.

2. Mix together the cracker crumbs and melted butter, and press into the base of the pan. Bake for 10 minutes, or until lightly browned. Let cool.

3. Beat the cream cheese until soft and smooth. Add the salt, cornstarch, and sugar, and beat for 1 minute.

4. Add the eggs and yolks gradually, beating well to combine. Stir in the vanilla extract and vanilla seeds, if using. Lightly whip the cream and fold half into the mixture. Refrigerate the remaining cream.

5. Pour the mix into the prepared pan and bake for 50 to 60 minutes, or until set at the edge but slightly soft in the center. Turn off the oven, leave the cake inside, and leave the door ajar. Cool in the oven for 30 minutes.

6. Remove the cheesecake and cool to room temperature. Remove from the pan, cover with foil, and refrigerate until cool. Cover the top with the remaining whipped cream and decorate with your favorite fruit.

Cherry Cheesecake

10–12 slices

2 cups/300g all-purpose flour, sifted
Scant 1 cup/100g confectioners' sugar
1⅓ sticks/150g sweet butter
6 egg yolks
2 tsp grated lemon peel
2 tbsp heavy whipping cream
1 cup/200g sugar
1lb 2oz/500g cream cheese
Pinch salt
3 tbsp cornstarch
2 eggs
1 cup/240ml sour cream
2 tsp vanilla extract
15oz/425g can cherries, drained

1. Grease a 9in/23cm springform cake pan. Sift the flour, less 3 tbsp, with the confectioners' sugar. Rub in 1¼ sticks/125g butter until the mixture resembles fine bread crumbs. Add 4 egg yolks, the peel, and heavy cream, and mix to form a dough. Wrap in baking parchment and refrigerate for 20 minutes. Preheat the oven to 375°F/190°C.

2. Roll the dough to ¼in/5mm thick. Line the base and three-quarters of the way up the sides of the pan. Prick the base all over with a fork. Freeze for 10 minutes.

3. When the pastry shell is firm, line with baking parchment and beans. Bake blind for 10 to 12 minutes, then remove the beans and bake for another 3 to 5 minutes.

4. Rub together the remaining flour, butter, and 2 tbsp sugar, and set aside this topping.

5. Beat the cream cheese until smooth. Add the salt, cornstarch, and remaining sugar, and beat for 1 minute. Gradually add the eggs and remaining yolks, beating well to combine. Stir in the sour cream and vanilla. Fold in the cherries and spoon into the pan.

6. Sprinkle with the topping. Bake for 50 to 55 minutes. After 20 minutes reduce the oven temperature to 300°F/150°C. Turn off the oven, leave the cheesecake inside to cool for 30 minutes. Refrigerate when completely cool.

White Chocolate Amaretto Cheesecake

*This creamy cake with its delicate
amaretto flavoring needs to be made
the day before eating—the perfect
dessert for entertaining.*

10–12 slices

16–18 Graham crackers
3–4 amaretti cookies
½ stick/50g butter, melted
½ tsp almond extract
½ tsp ground cinnamon

For the filling:
12oz/350g good quality white
  chocolate, melted
½ cup/120ml heavy cream
3 (8oz/225g) packages cream
  cheese, softened
⅓ cup/65g sugar
4 eggs
2 tbsp amaretto liqueur or ½ tsp
  almond extract
½ tsp vanilla extract

For the topping:
1¾ cups/400ml sour cream
¼ cup/50g sugar
1 tbsp amaretto or ½ tsp almond extract
White chocolate curls, to decorate

1. Preheat the oven to 350°F/180°C, and
grease a 9 x 3in/23 x 7.5cm springform cake
pan. Put the crackers and cookies into a
food processor and pulse into fine crumbs.
Add the butter, almond extract, and cinnamon,
and blend. Press the crumbs onto the base
and sides of the pan. Bake for 5 to 7 minutes.
Transfer the pan to a wire rack, and reduce
the temperature to 300°F/150°C.

2. To make the filling, melt the chocolate
and cream in a pan over low heat, stirring
until smooth. Set aside, stirring occasionally.

3. Using an electric mixer, beat the cream
cheese until smooth. Gradually add the
sugar, then each egg, beating well after each
addition. Slowly beat in the melted chocolate

mixture, the amaretto or almond extract, and the vanilla extract.

4. Turn into the prepared pan, place on a baking sheet, and bake for 45 to 55 minutes, or until the edge of the cake is firm, but the center is slightly soft. Transfer the pan to a wire rack, and increase the oven temperature to 400°F/200°C.

5. To make the topping, beat the sour cream, sugar, and amaretto or almond extract. Spread over the cheesecake. Return to the oven and bake for 5 to 7 minutes. Turn off the oven, but leave the cake inside for 1 hour. Transfer to a wire rack to cool. Run a sharp knife between the crust and the side of the cake pan to separate the two, but leave in the pan. Refrigerate, loosely covered, overnight.

6. To serve, unclip and remove the cheesecake. Transfer to a serving plate and decorate with white chocolate curls.

Classic Cheesecake with Blackberry Topping

6–8 slices

14 Graham crackers, crushed
5 tbsp/65g butter, melted
3 large eggs, separated
Scant 1 cup/175g sugar
1½ (8oz/225g) packages cream cheese
Generous ¾ cup/200ml sour cream
2 tbsp cornstarch
2 tsp vanilla extract
4 tsp grated lemon peel

For the topping:
1lb/450g blackberries
½ cup/100g sugar
4 tsp arrowroot
4 tbsp blackberry or cherry liqueur

1. Preheat the oven to 350°F/180°C. Grease a 9in/23cm springform cake pan and line the base with baking parchment. Mix the crackers and butter together and press evenly into the base of the pan.

2. Beat the egg yolks and half the sugar until light and fluffy. Add the cheese a little at a time, beating until smooth. Mix in the cream, cornstarch, vanilla extract, lemon peel, and remaining sugar.

3. In another bowl, beat the egg whites until stiff, then fold them into the mixture. Pour into the pan and bake for 1 to 1¼ hours, or until just set and golden on top. Run a knife around the inside of the pan, then cool in the oven with the door ajar.

4. For the topping cook the blackberries in 4 tbsp water for 5 minutes, or until the juices run and the berries are soft. Blend the arrowroot with the liqueur and stir into the fruit. Bring to a boil, then remove from the heat cool.

5. Remove the cheesecake from the pan and pour the blackberries and glaze over it. Refrigerate for 4 hours before serving.

Italian Ricotta Cheesecake

Ricotta cheese makes a light cheesecake. You could make a Graham cracker base as used for the New York Cheesecake on page 66.

10–12 slices

1½ lb/675g ricotta cheese
8oz/225g mascarpone cheese
¾ cup/150g sugar
2 tbsp cornstarch
4 eggs
2 tsp vanilla extract
¼ tsp ground cinnamon
2 tsp lemon peel
Pinch salt

1. Preheat the oven to 300°F/150°C, and grease a 9in/23cm springform cake pan.

2. Beat the ricotta and mascarpone together in a large bowl until smooth. Then stir in the sugar and cornstarch.

3. Gradually add the eggs beating well to combine. Stir in the vanilla extract, cinnamon, lemon peel, and salt, and pour the mixture into the prepared pan.

4. Bake for 50 to 60 minutes, or until just firm to the touch. Let cool to room temperature, cover with foil, and refrigerate thoroughly before serving.

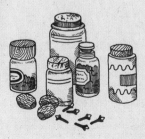

Marble Cheesecake

12–15 slices

7oz/200g Graham cracker crumbs
4 tbsp sweet butter, melted
3 (8oz/225g) packages cream cheese
Pinch salt
3 tbsp cornstarch
1 cup/200g sugar
2 eggs
2 egg yolks
2 tsp vanilla extract
2 cups/480ml heavy whipping cream
5oz/150g bittersweet chocolate, melted
4 tbsp unsweetened cocoa powder
2 tsp vanilla seeds

1. Preheat the oven to 300°F/150°C. Grease a 9in/23cm springform cake pan.

2. Mix together the cracker crumbs and melted butter, and press into the base of the prepared pan. Bake for 10 minutes, or until lightly browned, then let cool.

3. Beat the cheese until smooth. Add the salt, cornstarch, and sugar, and beat for 1 minute. Gradually add the eggs, beating to combine. Stir in the vanilla. Whip the cream, and fold into the mixture. Divide the mixture equally between two bowls. Add the melted chocolate and cocoa to one and mix well. Stir the vanilla seeds into the other bowl.

4. Spoon half the chocolate mixture into the pan then spoon the vanilla mix over the top. Spoon over the remaining chocolate mix and draw a knife through the mix to create a swirled marble effect.

5. Bake for 55 to 60 minutes, or until set at the edge but slightly soft in the center. Turn off the oven and cool in the oven for 45 minutes.

6. Remove the cheesecake from the oven and cool to room temperature. Remove from the pan, cover with foil and refrigerate until cold.

Banana Toffee Cheesecake

A classic, rich cheesecake treat that's as popular with adults as it is with hungry children.

10–12 slices

1½ cups/225g all-purpose flour
Pinch salt
Scant 1 stick/100g butter, diced
¼ cup/50g sugar
3–4 tbsp cold water

For the filling:
4oz/115g bittersweet chocolate,
   broken into pieces, plus extra
   to decorate
14oz/400g can sweetened
   condensed milk
3 large ripe but firm bananas
Juice ½ lemon
2½ cups/250g mascarpone cheese
Scant ⅔ cup/150ml heavy whipping
   cream, lightly whipped

1. Sift the flour into a bowl with the salt. Using your fingertips, rub the butter into the flour until the mixture resembles coarse bread crumbs. Stir in the sugar. Add 3 tbsp cold water and, using a narrow spatula, start to bring the dough together, adding a little more water, if necessary. Turn the dough onto a lightly floured surface and knead briefly, until the dough is smooth. Form into a neat ball and wrap in plastic wrap. Refrigerate for 20 minutes.

2. Roll the dough into a rough circle at least 2in/5cm larger than a loose-bottomed 9in/23cm fluted tart pan set on a baking sheet. Gently roll the dough onto the rolling pin, then unroll it over the pan to cover. Carefully press the pastry into the edge of the pan, removing any overhanging dough with a knife. Prick the base all over with a fork. Refrigerate for 20 minutes. Meanwhile, preheat the oven to 400°F/200°C. Line the pastry shell with baking parchment and fill with dried beans. Transfer to the oven and bake for 12 minutes. Remove the dried beans and parchment and cook for 10 to 12 minutes, or until golden. Remove from the oven and let cool. Carefully brush off any crumbs from inside the pastry shell.

3. Melt the chocolate in a bowl set over a pan of simmering water. Using a pastry brush, paint the chocolate onto the pastry shell to cover completely. Refrigerate until set.

4. Meanwhile, pour the can of sweetened condensed milk into a heatproof bowl over a pan of boiling water. Simmer over low heat for 1 to 1½ hours, or until thick and caramel-colored. Beat until smooth. Remove the bowl from the heat and let cool.

5. To assemble the cheesecake, thickly slice the bananas and drizzle with the lemon juice. Set aside. Beat the mascarpone cheese until softened, then stir in the cream. Carefully fold the cream and toffee mixtures together, but don't overmix—leave them marbled. Fold in the bananas, then spoon the mixture into the pastry shell. Grate the remaining chocolate over the top.

Dark Chocolate Cheesecake

*A fabulous cake for chocoholics. Use
the best quality chocolate you can find.*

12-15 slices

7oz/200g Graham cracker crumbs
4 tbsp sweet butter, melted
3 (8oz/225g) packages cream cheese
Pinch salt
3 tbsp cornstarch
1 cup/200g sugar
2 eggs
2 egg yolks
2 tsp vanilla extract
1½ cups/350ml heavy whipping cream
½ cup/120ml sour cream
10oz/275g bittersweet chocolate, melted
6 tbsp unsweetened cocoa powder
2 tbsp chocolate shards
1 tbsp unsweetened cocoa powder,
   for dusting

1. Preheat the oven to 300°F/150°C.
Grease a 9in/23cm springform cake pan.

2. Mix together the cracker crumbs and
melted butter, and press into the base of the
pan. Bake for 10 minutes, or until lightly
browned, then let cool.

3. Beat the cream cheese until soft and
smooth. Add the salt, cornstarch, and sugar,
and beat for 1 minute. Gradually add the eggs
and yolks, beating well to combine. Stir in the
vanilla extract. Lightly whip the cream. Fold
the cream and sour cream into the mixture.

4. Add the melted chocolate and cocoa, and
mix well to combine. Pour the cheesecake
mixture into the prepared pan and bake for
55 to 60 minutes, or until set at the edge
but slightly soft in the center. Turn off the
oven and cool in the oven for 45 minutes.

5. Remove the cheesecake from the oven
and cool to room temperature. Remove
from the pan, cover with foil, and refrigerate
until cold. Decorate with shards of chocolate
and dust with cocoa before serving.

CHAPTER FIVE

Dessert Cakes

Angel Food Cake

A truly magnificent feat in the art of cake-making, this cake is held together almost purely by air.

6–8 slices

⅓ cup/50g all-purpose flour
1 tbsp cornstarch
1 cup/200g sugar, plus 2 tbsp
7 egg whites
¾ tsp cream of tartar
Pinch salt
1½ tsp vanilla extract

For the frosting:
2 egg whites
2⅓ cups/350g sugar
¼ tsp cream of tartar
2 tbsp toasted chopped pistachio nuts,
   plus extra to decorate

1. Preheat the oven to 350°F/180°C. Sift the flour and cornstarch together. Add ⅓ cup/65g of the sugar and sift together twice.

2. Beat the egg whites until foamy. Add the cream of tartar and salt and beat until stiff.

3. Beat the remaining sugar into the egg whites until stiff and glossy. Beat in the vanilla extract.

4. Fold in the flour, then spoon the mixture into a 9in/23cm springform tube pan. The mixture should come to the top of the pan. Level the top and bake for 45 to 50 minutes, or until lightly golden and spongy to the touch. Remove from the oven and invert onto a wire rack. Cool in the pan.

5. To make the frosting, put all the ingredients into a bowl, add 4 tbsp water, and set the bowl over a pan of hot water. Beat with a hand-held mixer for 10 to 12 minutes, or until thick.

6. Run a knife around the side of the pan and remove. Spread the frosting over the top. Finish with a sprinkle of pistachio nuts.

Orange Chiffon Cake

Light and flavorful, serve this citrus cake as a dessert with fresh fruit.

12–14 slices

1½ cups/225g cake flour
2 tsp baking powder
Pinch salt
1½ cups/300g sugar
½ cup/120ml safflower oil
4 egg yolks
¾ cup/180ml orange juice
2 tbsp orange peel
1 tsp vanilla extract
3 eggs, separated
Pinch cream of tartar

1. Preheat the oven to 325°F/160°C. Lightly grease a 10in/25cm Bundt pan.

2. Combine the flour, baking powder, salt, and sugar in a bowl and mix well.

3. Make a well in the center and pour in the oil, egg yolks, orange juice and peel, and vanilla extract. Beat for 1 minute, or until smooth.

4. In a separate bowl beat the egg whites until they start to form soft peaks. Add the cream of tartar and whisk until stiff peaks form. Fold the egg whites into the batter using a balloon whisk.

5. Pour the batter into the prepared pan and bake for 55 minutes, or until the cake is firm to the touch. Invert the cake on the neck of a bottle and cool the cake completely before removing from the pan.

Peach Cake

The peach halves in this recipe keep the cake moist and fruity—enjoy with a large cup of coffee at any time of the day.

10 slices

1½ sticks/175g sweet butter
Scant 1 cup/175g sugar
3 eggs
2 cups/200g ground almonds
⅔ cup/100g cake flour
2 tsp vanilla extract
15oz/425g can small peach
    halves, drained
1 tbsp confectioners' sugar

1. Preheat the oven to 350°F/180°C. Grease and base line a 9in/23cm round cake pan.

2. Cream the butter and sugar until pale and fluffy, and then gradually add the eggs, beating well between each addition.

3. Stir in the ground almonds, flour, and vanilla extract.

4. Spoon the batter into the prepared pan and smooth over the surface. Place the peach halves evenly over the surface of the cake batter.

5. Bake the cake for 35 to 40 minutes. Remove from the oven and let cool. Dust with confectioners' sugar before serving.

Simple Almond Cake

This light cake is packed with ground almonds and is delicious served with fresh fruit and whipped cream for added luxury.

6–8 slices

2½ cups/250g ground almonds
2 tbsp all-purpose flour, sifted
7 large egg whites
1 cup/200g sugar, plus 2 tbsp
2 tbsp orange liqueur
Scant ⅔ cup/150ml whipping cream, whipped
6oz/175g strawberries, sliced
Confectioners' sugar, for dusting

1. Preheat the oven to 350°F/180°C, and grease and line a 9in/23cm springform cake pan. Sift the almonds and flour together into a bowl and set aside. Beat the egg whites in another bowl until stiff. Keep beating while gradually adding the sugar until the mixture is smooth and glossy.

2. Gently fold in the flour and almond mixture. Spoon into the pan and bake for 25 to 30 minutes, or until golden and spongy to the touch.

3. Cool in the pan and then turn out and slice through horizontally. Drizzle the orange liqueur over each half. Spread one half with the whipped cream and top with the sliced strawberries. Top with the second half and dust with confectioners' sugar before serving.

Sponge Cake Roll with Lemon Cream

This sponge roll has a splendid mascarpone and citrus filling. Jelly, buttercream, or cream and fruit could be used for the filling, if you prefer.

6 slices

4 large eggs
½ cup/100g sugar, plus extra for dusting
⅔ cup/100g all-purpose flour

For the filling:
2¼ cups/225g mascarpone cheese
1 tsp grated lemon peel
1 tbsp fresh lemon juice
2 tbsp fresh orange juice
4 tbsp confectioners' sugar

1. Preheat the oven to 425°F/220°C, and grease and line a 9 x 13in/23 x 33cm jelly roll pan with baking parchment.

2. Beat the eggs and sugar with a hand-held mixer in a large bowl until thick and frothy and the beaters leave a trail when lifted out of the mixture.

3. Sift and fold in the flour in three batches using a large metal spoon. Pour the mixture into the prepared pan and spread into the corners. Bake for about 10 minutes, or until golden brown and the top springs back when pressed lightly.

4. While the cake is cooking lay a sheet of baking parchment on a surface and sprinkle liberally with sugar.

5. Holding the lining paper and pan edges, turn the cake out onto the baking parchment. Peel the lining paper from the cake. Trim the edges and score a cut 1in/2.5cm in from one of the shorter ends. Roll up the cake with baking parchment and let cool on a wire rack.

6. Beat the filling ingredients together. Carefully unroll the jelly roll and spread with the filling. Roll up and serve in slices.

Strawberry Cake with Slivered Almonds

This delightful strawberry cake is a great summertime treat. Substitute best quality strawberry compote in place of the fresh strawberries, if you prefer.

8–10 slices

2¼ sticks/250g sweet butter
1¼ cups/250g sugar
2 eggs
1 tsp vanilla extract
Pinch salt
4 tbsp sour cream
1 tsp baking soda
1½ cups/225g all-purpose flour
1 cup/100g ground almonds

For the frosting:
1½ cups/350ml heavy whipping cream
2 tbsp confectioners' sugar
1 tsp grated lemon peel
4 tbsp sour cream
4 tbsp toasted slivered almonds
1lb/450g strawberries, halved and sliced

1. Preheat the oven to 350°F/180°C. Grease and base line a 9in/23cm round cake pan.

2. Cream together the butter and the sugar until light and fluffy. Gradually add the eggs, beating well after each addition. Stir in the vanilla extract, salt, and sour cream.

3. Sift the baking soda with the flour and then fold into the egg mixture with the ground almonds.

4. Pour the batter into the prepared pan and bake for 30 to 35 minutes, or until golden and firm to the touch. Remove from the pan and let cool on a wire rack.

5. To make the frosting, lightly whip the cream. Add the confectioners' sugar, the lemon peel, and sour cream. Spread over the cake. Press the slivered almonds around the sides, and top with the strawberry pieces. Refrigerate until ready to serve.

Raspberry Soufflé Gâteau

A light but sharp-tasting dessert topped with fresh berries.

8–10 slices

⅔ stick/75g sweet butter
2 cups/200g Graham crackers, crushed
¼ cup/50g sugar
4 cups/400g frozen raspberries
1 tbsp or 3 leaves gelatin
1¼ cups/300ml heavy whipping cream
3 egg whites
Pinch cream of tartar
½ cup/100g sugar
¼ cup/50g fresh raspberries, to decorate

1. Preheat the oven to 350°F/180°C.

2. Melt the butter and stir in the crushed crackers and sugar in a large bowl. Press onto the base of a 9in/23cm springform cake pan and bake for 10 minutes. Cool and set aside.

3. Combine the raspberries with 3 tbsp water in a pan and simmer gently until they are soft. Process the mixture in a food processor or blender for 30 seconds, and then strain to remove the seeds.

4. Soften and dissolve the gelatin. If using leaf gelatin, soak in cold water and squeeze out the excess. If using powdered gelatin, sprinkle onto hot water. Dissolve in a bowl over a pan of simmering water. Stir into the raspberry pulp. Let cool. Whip the cream until soft peaks form and fold through the raspberry pulp.

5. Beat the egg whites until soft peaks form. Add the cream of tartar and half the sugar. Beat until stiff peaks form, and then whisk in the remaining sugar. Fold the whites through the raspberry and cream mixture, and spoon onto the prepared crust. Chill for 2 to 3 hours, or until set.

6. Decorate with fresh raspberries.

Praline Layer Cake

*Toasted pecan nuts make a truly
delicious praline.*

8–10 slices

4oz/115g bittersweet chocolate
½ stick/50g sweet butter
2 cups/400g sugar
2 egg yolks
½ cup/120ml milk
1⅓ cups/200g cake flour
Pinch salt
½ tsp baking soda
1 tsp vanilla extract

For the filling:
1 cup/200g sugar
¼ cup/50g toasted chopped pecan nuts
1 cup/240ml heavy whipping cream

1. Preheat the oven to 325°F/160°C. Grease
and base line two 8in/20cm round pans.

2. Melt the chocolate and butter in a large
bowl set over a pan of gently simmering
water, then let cool to room temperature.
Stir in the sugar. Add the egg yolks and half
the milk and mix well.

3. Add the flour, salt, and baking soda, and
beat for 1 minute with an electric mixer.
Blend in the remaining milk and vanilla
extract. Pour into the prepared pans.

4. Bake for 25 to 30 minutes, or until just
firm to the touch. Remove from the pans
and let cool on a wire rack.

5. To make the filling, melt the sugar gently
in a heavy bottomed pan. Lightly oil a piece
of foil on a baking sheet or a piece of
marble. When the sugar is golden, stir in the
pecans. Pour onto the oiled surface. When
cool break into small pieces and put into a
food processor. Blend to a fine powder.

6. Whip the cream and fold into the nut
powder. Fill and top the cake with the
cream frosting. Cover and refrigerate
before serving.

Ice Cream Cake

A simple angel cake is made extra special with vanilla ice cream, succulent peaches, and rich, ruby-red Melba sauce.

10–12 slices

1½ cups/300g sugar
1 cup/150g cake flour
8 medium egg whites, at room
   temperature
1¼ tsp cream of tartar
Pinch salt
1 tsp almond extract
½ tsp vanilla extract
6–8 maraschino cherries (optional)
Confectioners' sugar, for dusting

For the Melba sauce:
¾ cup/150g sugar
2 cups/225g fresh raspberries, puréed
   and chilled

For the filling:
Scoops of ice cream, preferably vanilla,
   enough to fill the center core
1 (1lb/450g) can yellow peaches,
   drained

1. Preheat the oven to 350°F/180°C. Sift the sugar twice. In a separate bowl, sift the flour four times. Set both aside.

2. Beat the egg whites in another bowl until frothy. Add the cream of tartar and salt, and continue to beat until the mixture forms soft peaks. Sprinkle 2 tbsp of sugar over the egg white peaks and beat until blended. Repeat the process until the sugar is used up.

3. Beat in the almond and vanilla extracts. With a rubber spatula, fold in the flour, ¼ cup/40g at a time. Cut the cherries into quarters, if using, and fold into the batter. Spoon the batter into an ungreased 9in/23cm fluted ring mold. Cut through the mixture with a knife to get rid of any air bubbles, and level off. Bake in the center of the oven for 40 to 60 minutes, or until the top turns light brown.

4. Remove from the oven, invert onto a wire rack, and let cool in the pan for 1 hour. Run a sharp knife around the edges of the mold to loosen the cake before inverting onto a serving plate. Dust the cake with confectioners' sugar before serving.

5. To make the Melba sauce, boil the sugar and ½ cup/120ml water for 10 minutes. Cool, then add the chilled berry purée. Pass through a fine strainer and refrigerate again.

6. To serve, fill the center recess of the cake with the ice cream and canned peaches. Pour some of the sauce over the ice cream, taking care to avoid soaking the cake, and serve the rest separately.

Variation:
Use mint ice cream and dust the top of the cake with confectioners' sugar or unsweetened cocoa powder. Serve with fresh strawberries and a hot chocolate sauce.

CHAPTER SIX

· · · · · · · · · · ·

Special Occasion Cakes

Strawberry Shortcake

8 slices

2⅔ cups/400g cake flour
1½ tbsp baking powder
¼ tsp salt
⅔ stick/75g sweet chilled butter,
  cut into small pieces
½ cup/100g sugar, plus extra for
  sprinkling
1 cup/240ml buttermilk, plus extra
  for brushing
1 cup/240ml heavy whipping cream
3 tbsp confectioners' sugar, plus extra
  for dusting
1 tsp vanilla extract
1lb/450g strawberries, halved

1. Preheat the oven to 375°F/190°C.
Grease and flour a baking sheet. Sift together
the flour, baking powder, and salt. Rub the
chilled butter into the flour until the mixture
forms fine bread crumbs.

2. Mix ⅔ cup of sugar with the buttermilk,
and pour into the flour mixture. Mix to form
a smooth dough, but do not overwork at
this stage. Turn out the dough onto a lightly
floured surface and divide into two balls, one
slightly larger than the other. Roll out to
¾in/2cm thick.

3. Place the circles on the prepared sheet.
Brush off any excess flour. Brush tops with
milk and sprinkle with sugar. Bake for 20 to
25 minutes, or until golden.

4. Cool on a wire rack. Whip the cream,
and add the confectioners' sugar and the
vanilla extract.

5. Gently heat half the strawberries in a
pan with 2 tablespoons of water and the
remaining sugar for 2 to 3 minutes to
soften the fruit.

6. Spoon ¾ of the cream onto the larger of
the cooled disks and spoon over the warm
strawberries and juice. Top with the other
disk, cream, and remaining strawberries.
Serve immediately.

Lady Baltimore

Billowy clouds of fruit and nut frosting top this light and delicious sponge cake.

12 slices

2¼ sticks/250g sweet butter, softened
1¼ cups/250g sugar
2 tsp vanilla extract
2 cups/300g all-purpose flour
1 tbsp baking powder
¼ tsp salt
1 cup/240ml milk
6 egg whites

For the frosting:
2 cups/400g sugar
2 tbsp corn syrup
4 egg whites
Pinch cream of tartar
½ cup/75g raisins
½ cup/50g chopped pecan nuts
½ cup/75g chopped candied cherries

1. Preheat the oven to 350°F/180°C. Grease and flour three 9in/23cm round cake pans.

2. Cream the butter and 1 cup/200g sugar and half the vanilla extract. Beat until light and fluffy.

3. Sift together the flour, baking powder, and salt. Add the flour and milk alternately to the creamed mixture.

4. Beat the egg whites until soft peaks form, then add ¼ cup/50g sugar and beat until the whites are stiff. Add one-third of the whites to the cake mix to lighten it and then fold through the rest. Pour the batter into the prepared pans.

5. Bake for 25 to 30 minutes, or until just firm to the touch. Remove from the pans and cool.

6. To make the frosting, put the sugar in a medium, heavy pan with the corn syrup and 6 tbsp water. Stir to dissolve the sugar over medium heat. Cook the sugar to medium ball stage, 245°F/118°C, without stirring. Start to beat the whites and the cream of tartar in a bowl before the sugar reaches medium ball. When the sugar has reached temperature pour the syrup steadily into the whites, beating constantly. Continue to beat for 5 minutes, or until the frosting is thick and creamy.

7. Let the frosting cool then stir in the raisins, pecans, cherries, and remaining vanilla extract. Fill and frost the cake both on the top and sides.

Valentine Sponge Hearts

These dainty sponge hearts, decorated with sugar flowers, will look pretty and taste delightful to finish a special evening's meal.

6–8 hearts

1½ sticks/175g sweet butter, softened
2¼ cups/450g sugar
2 tsp vanilla extract
1½ cups/225g all-purpose flour
2 tsp baking powder
Pinch salt
⅔ cup/160ml milk
4 egg whites
2 tbsp confectioners' sugar
6–8 piped sugar flowers, to decorate

1. Preheat the oven to 350°F/180°C. Grease and flour six to eight small heart-shaped molds or a 9 x 13in/23 x 33cm pan.

2. Cream the butter, 1¾ cups/350g of the sugar, and the vanilla extract. Beat until light and fluffy.

3. Sift together the flour, baking powder, and salt. Add the flour to the creamed mixture alternately with the milk.

4. Beat the egg whites until soft peaks form, then add the remaining sugar and beat until the whites are stiff. Add one-third of the whites to the cake mixture to lighten it and then fold in the rest.

5. Pour the batter into the prepared molds or pan and bake for 12 to 15 minutes, or until just firm to the touch. Remove and cool.

6. If you have one layer of sponge use a heart-shaped cutter to cut out six to eight hearts.

7. Use a small heart-shaped stencil and dust the hearts with confectioners' sugar. Decorate with piped sugar flowers.

Golden Buttercream Cake

Rich and buttery, this cake is an anytime cake. Eat and enjoy!

10 slices

1⅔ cups/250g cake flour
2 tsp baking powder
Pinch salt
2 sticks/225g sweet butter
1¼ cups/250g sugar
4 eggs
1 tsp vanilla extract

For the frosting:
1 stick/125g butter
1 tsp vanilla extract
Scant 2 cups/200g confectioners' sugar, sifted
3–4 drops yellow food coloring

1. Preheat the oven to 350°F/180°C. Grease and base line two 8in/20cm round cake pans.

2. Sift together the flour, baking powder, and salt.

3. Beat the butter until pale and fluffy. Add the sugar and beat for another 2 minutes. Gradually add the eggs, beating well between each addition. Add the vanilla extract and stir in the dry ingredients.

4. Pour the batter into the prepared pans and bake for 30 to 35 minutes, or until golden and firm to the touch. Remove from the pans and let cool on wire racks.

5. Beat the butter and vanilla extract until pale and fluffy then add the sifted confectioners' sugar. Add the yellow food coloring and beat well. Fill and frost the cake.

Coconut Cream Cake

A tasty classic—add to the kids' lunch boxes or indulge yourself.

6–8 slices

1¼ sticks/125g sweet butter, softened
¾ cup/150g sugar
1 cup/240ml buttermilk
1 tsp vanilla extract
1⅓ cups/200g all-purpose flour
1 tsp baking powder
½ tsp baking soda
Pinch salt
1 cup/100g flaked coconut
4 egg whites

1. Preheat the oven to 350°F/180°C. Grease and base line a 9in/23cm round cake pan.

2. Cream together the butter and sugar, and then mix in the buttermilk and vanilla extract. Sift the flour, baking powder, baking soda, and salt together and then stir into the butter mixture. Add the coconut, less 2 tbsp, and combine well.

3. Beat the egg whites stiffly and then add one-third to the cake mixture. Stir in to lighten the mixture then fold in the remainder. Pour the batter into the pan, and sprinkle with the reserved 2 tbsp coconut. Bake for 30 to 35 minutes, or until firm to the touch and golden in color. Remove from the pan and let cool.

Icebox Cake

For this simple and quick dessert, frozen raspberries are used straight from the icebox. Chill the cake well before serving.

8 slices

⅔ stick/75g sweet butter
2 cups/200g crushed Graham crackers
¼ cup/50g brown sugar

For the filling:
6oz/175g raspberry gelatin mix
3 cups/300g frozen raspberries
20 large pink marshmallows
4 tbsp milk
2 cups/480ml heavy whipping cream

1. Preheat the oven to 350°F/180°C.

2. Melt the butter and stir in the crushed crackers and sugar. Press onto the base of a 9in/23cm springform cake pan and bake for 10 minutes. Cool and set aside.

3. Dissolve the raspberry gelatin in ½ cup/120ml boiling water and stir in the frozen raspberries. Pour onto the prepared base.

4. Melt the marshmallows with the milk in a pan over low heat. Pour into a bowl and let cool.

5. Whip the cream lightly and fold through the cooled marshmallow mixture. Spoon the marshmallow cream on top of the raspberry jelly. Refrigerate for 2 to 3 hours before serving.

Rum Cake

This cake can double as a dessert. Serve it warm with pan-fried bananas and vanilla ice cream for a sensational finish to a meal.

8–10 slices

1¾ sticks/200g sweet butter, softened
1¼ cups/250g brown sugar
2 eggs
1⅔ cups/250g all-purpose flour
½ tsp baking powder
1 tsp ground allspice
Pinch salt
3 tbsp dark rum

For the filling:
¼ cup/50g sugar
3 tbsp rum
3 tbsp butter

1. Preheat the oven to 350°F/180°C. Grease and base line a 2lb/900g loaf pan.

2. Beat the butter until pale and creamy and then add the brown sugar and beat for another 3 to 4 minutes.

3. Gradually add the eggs and beat well. Sift together the flour, baking powder, allspice, and salt. Fold into the creamed mixture with the rum.

4. Pour the batter into the prepared pan and bake for 50 to 55 minutes, or until the cake is firm to the touch and a skewer inserted into the center of the cake comes out clean.

5. To make the filling, dissolve the sugar with the rum, butter, and 2 tbsp water in a pan.

6. Using a toothpick, prick the top of the cake lightly and pour over the rum syrup. Serve warm or cold.

Baked Alaska Birthday Cake

*Dim the lights, and light the candles;
This is an all-time favorite celebration
cake, and the fresh raspberries make
it extra special.*

6–8 slices

1½ sticks/175g sweet butter
¾ cup/175g granulated sugar
3 eggs, beaten
1 tsp vanilla extract
1½ cups/175g self-rising flour, sifted
12oz/350g raspberry jelly
1½ cups/225g raspberries
4 egg whites
1 cup/225g sugar
8 scoops vanilla or your favorite
  ice cream
Candles or sparklers, to decorate

1. Preheat the oven to 350°F/180°C, and
grease and base line an 8in/20cm cake pan.

2. Cream the butter and sugar in a large
mixing bowl. Add the eggs and vanilla
extract and beat well. Fold in the flour.
Spoon into the prepared cake pan. Level
the top of the batter and cook for 30 to
35 minutes, or until risen and golden. Turn
out and let cool on a wire rack.

3. Preheat the oven to 425°F/220°C.
Split the sponge in half horizontally. Place
the base sponge on a baking sheet and
spread with jelly. Place the second sponge
disk on top. Arrange the raspberries on top
of the sponge.

4. Place the egg whites in a large bowl and
beat until they form stiff peaks. Beat in the
sugar, a spoonful at a time.

5. Place scoops of ice cream over the
raspberries to cover. Spread the meringue
mixture over the ice cream and sides of the
sponge so that everything is covered.

6. Bake for 8 to 10 minutes. Remove from
the oven, decorate with birthday candles or
sparklers (optional) and serve immediately.

Red Velvet Cake

Deep, dark layers of sponge are covered in creamy white frosting for this truly impressive cake.

8–10 slices

⅔ stick/75g sweet butter, softened
1½ cups/300g sugar
2 eggs
1 tsp vanilla extract
1½ cups/225g all-purpose flour
3 tbsp unsweetened cocoa powder
1½ tsp baking soda
Pinch salt
1 tbsp red paste food color
½ cup/120ml buttermilk
1 tbsp vinegar

For the frosting:
⅔ stick/75g sweet butter, softened
1 (8oz/225g) package cream
  cheese, softened
1lb/450g confectioners' sugar
1 tsp vanilla extract
1 cup/100g chopped pecan nuts

1. Preheat the oven to 350°F/180°C. Grease and flour two 9in/23cm round cake pans.

2. Cream the butter and the sugar, and beat in the eggs and the vanilla extract.

3. Sift together the flour, cocoa powder, baking soda, and salt into a separate bowl. Stir the food color into the buttermilk. Alternately add the flour and buttermilk to the creamed mixture. Stir in the vinegar.

4. Pour into the prepared pans and bake for 30 to 35 minutes. Remove from the oven and let cool for 10 minutes in the pans. Remove and cool on a wire rack.

5. To make the frosting, beat together the butter and the cream cheese. Beat in the confectioners' sugar and vanilla extract, and then stir in the pecans. Fill and frost the cake when it is cool.

Rocky Road Cake

Marshmallows, walnuts, and chocolate caramels make a rich frosting for this all-time favorite cake.

10 slices

1½ cups/225g cake flour
2 tsp baking powder
4 tbsp unsweetened cocoa powder
Pinch salt
2 sticks/225g sweet butter
1¼ cups/250g sugar
4 eggs
6 tbsp buttermilk
2 tsp vanilla extract

For the filling:
35 chocolate-covered caramels
3 tbsp milk
3 cups/125g marshmallows
1 cup/100g chopped walnuts

1. Preheat the oven to 350°F/180°C. Grease and base line two 8in/20cm round pans.

2. Sift together the flour, baking powder, cocoa powder, and salt.

3. Beat the butter until pale and fluffy. Add the sugar and beat for another 2 minutes. Gradually add the eggs, beating well between each addition, and then stir in the buttermilk and vanilla extract.

4. Stir in the dry ingredients. Pour the batter into the prepared pans and bake for 30 to 35 minutes, or until firm to the touch. Remove from the pans and let cool on wire racks. Cut small slits into the top of each layer.

5. Melt the caramels with the milk and ½ cup/120g marshmallows. Put one cake layer on a plate and pour over half the chocolate mix. Sprinkle over half the nuts.

6. Place the second cake layer on top and pour over the remaining chocolate frosting. Sprinkle with the remaining nuts and marshmallows. Serve.

Index

Glossary

US:UK terms are given below for foods that have different names in the UK:

U.S.	British	U.S.	British
2% milk	semi-skimmed milk	heavy cream	double cream
all-purpose flour	plain flour	jelly	jam
almond extract	almond essence	light cream	single cream
baking soda	bicarbonate of soda	molasses	black treacle
		packed brown sugar	muscovado sugar
bittersweet chocolate	dark chocolate	plastic wrap	clingfilm
cake pan	cake tin	self-rising flour	self-raising flour
confectioners' sugar	icing sugar	sugar	caster sugar
cornstarch	cornflour	sweet butter	unsalted butter
golden raisins	sultanas	vanilla extract	vanilla essence
Graham crackers	digestive biscuits	whole wheat flour	wholemeal flour

Picture Credits

Pages 7, 22, 27, 35, 38, 43, 46, 69, 74, 85, 88, 97, 100 © Cephas/Stockfood.
Page 11 © Eaglemoss Consumer Publications/Anthony Blake Photo Library.
Page 19 © S. Lee Studios/Anthony Blake Photo Library.
Pages 53, 56, 79 © Martin Brigdale/Anthony Blake Photo Library.
Page 107 © Andrew Sydenham/Anthony Blake Photo Library.